Participant's Manual

BPR (Best Possible Results) Activity:
Move students from the attitude of

I CAN'T TO I CAN'T YET or I CAN

LOCK

KEY

MORAL KOMBAT 10
SMOKE FREE 4 ME
Tobacco Deterrence

Participant's Manual
1st Edition
Revised September 2019

Author & Creator: Carrie D. Marchant, M.A., Criminology Co-Author & Editor of Edition #1 & 3: Debbie Dunn, M.A.

1st Edition Editor: Kay Augustine, ED.S.

Disclaimer

Although the information and recommendations contained in this publication were compiled from sources believed to be reliable, the Tobacco Education, Awareness and Intervention for Teens Program makes no guarantee as to, and assumes no responsibility for the correctness, sufficiency, or completeness of such information or recommendations. Other or additional methods may be used under particular circumstances.

CHARACTER COUNTS!®️ and The Six Pillars of Character are service marks of the Josephson Institute and are used in this publication by permission of the Josephson Institute of Ethics, 9841 Airport Blvd., Suite 300, Los Angeles, CA 90045. www.charactercounts.org.

What is MORAL KOMBAT about?

Life isn't always easy, and making decisions isn't always easy either. You hear people say, "If I just had a set of directions to help me get through life…to help me make decisions…life would be so much easier." Well, that's kind of what MK10 is about. We realize no one, no book, no program or manual could be close to having all the answers –that's for sure! But we have some strategies that, if you choose to apply them, will bring profound change to your life.

MK created by Carrie D. Marchant

The creator of MORAL KOMBAT lived a very chaotic life as a child in a tremendously dysfunctional home. She then went on to live a tumultuous life as a troubled teen. She knows firsthand what it feels like to be misunderstood, feel that her options are limited, and just how difficult it is to make good decisions, especially when you're faced with so many obstacles.

It wasn't easy, but she turned her life around. She went to college and decided to spend every moment she could with teens, studying their behaviors and helping in any way possible. She is now a criminologist. She spends most of her time working with teens and their families, plus expanding the MORAL KOMBAT programs—which have proven successful in thousands of teens' lives. Co-author of this program, as of 2015, is Debbie Dunn. She facilitated many of the East Tennessee MORAL KOMBAT classes.

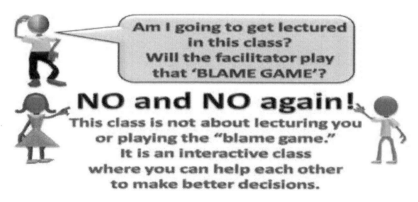

Am I going to get lectured in this class? Will the facilitator play that 'BLAME GAME'?

NO and NO again! This class is not about lecturing you or playing the "blame game." It is an interactive class where you can help each other to make better decisions.

Group Values based on The Six Pillars of Character® from CHARACTER COUNTS!®

BLUE | YELLOW | GREEN | ORANGE | RED | PURPLE

THE SIX PILLARS OF CHARACTER®

The Six Pillars of Character®: Trustworthiness, Respect, Responsibility, Fairness, Caring and Citizenship.

T = Trustworthiness
R = Respect
R = Responsibility
F = Fairness
C = Caring
C = Citizenship

Students generate a list of Group Values based on The Six Pillars of Character® from the CHARACTER COUNTS!® program

GROUP VALUES	
Trustworthiness	
Respect	
Responsibility	
Fairness	
Caring	
Citizenship	

What do you notice about The Six Pillars of Character® acronym?

❶ **Trustworthiness**

 During your tobacco use, in what ways are other people around you expecting you to demonstrate TRUSTWORTHINESS?

 During other people's tobacco use and/or anti-tobacco stance, in what ways are you expecting other people to demonstrate TRUSTWORTHINESS?

---

❷ Respect

 During your tobacco use, in what ways are other people around you expecting you to demonstrate RESPECT?

 During other people's tobacco use and/or anti-tobacco stance, in what ways are you expecting other people to demonstrate RESPECT?

❸ Responsibility

 During your tobacco use, in what ways are other people around you expecting you to demonstrate RESPONSIBILITY?

 During other people's tobacco use and/or anti-tobacco stance, in what ways are you expecting other people to demonstrate RESPONSIBILITY?

❹ Fairness

 During your tobacco use, in what ways are other people around you expecting you to demonstrate FAIRNESS?

 During other people's tobacco use and/or anti-tobacco stance, in what ways are you expecting other people to demonstrate FAIRNESS?

❺ Caring

 During your tobacco use, in what ways are other people around you expecting you to demonstrate CARING?

 During other people's tobacco use and/or anti-tobacco stance, in what ways are you expecting other people to demonstrate CARING?

❻ Citizenship

 During your tobacco use, in what ways are other people around you expecting you to demonstrate CITIZENSHIP?

 During other people's tobacco use and/or anti-tobacco stance, in what ways are you expecting other people to demonstrate CITIZENSHIP?

Introduce yourself during the WEB OF LIFE Activity

Collective Group Activity: We are about to participate in a really fun activity called "The Web of Life." Before we do, let's discuss the following quote by Chief Seattle. Predict how you think this quote might apply to you and to us as a group.

> "Humankind has not woven the web of life.
> We are but one thread within it.
> Whatever we do to the web, we do to ourselves.
> All things are bound together. All things connect."
> – Chief Seattle

Introductory Activity:

WEB OF LIFE

Beginning with the facilitator, you will, one at a time, wrap the end of a ball of string around your forefinger, and then answer these 5 questions:

WEB OF LIFE

1. My name is _____.
2. My school is called _____.
3. My age is _____.
4. **My tobacco issues are the following:_____.**
5. **Relate how you got caught and what were the consequences. _____**

> **"Become the master of difficult situations by refusing the assistance of those weak in character. Rely on your own strength of character."**
> **--I Ching**

Collective Group Activity: Look at the quote from I Ching.

1. Let's get a volunteer to read it.
2. Thinking about the tools you use and used to solve conflicts and stressors, how would you describe the meaning of this quotation?

> **"Obstacles don't have to stop you. If you run into a wall, don't turn around and give up. Figure out how to climb it, go through it, or work around it."**
> **--Michael Jordan**

Collective Group Activity: Look at the quote from Michael Jordan.

3. Let's get a volunteer to read it.
4. Thinking about the tools you use and used to solve conflicts and stressors, how would you describe the meaning of this quotation?

Collective Group Activity:

Which STAKEHOLDERS were positively or negatively impacted by your decisions?

Collective Group Activity:

With you in the center of this web, picture the people around you who were either positively or negatively affected by the action or actions that got you placed on probation or directed to take this MORAL KOMBAT class.

These people are your **STAKEHOLDERS**. They were invested and/or impacted by your life-decisions.

During the Web of Life activity, you shared the decision you made that got you placed on probation. Like the quote states on the previous page, "Your every action impacts your **STAKEHOLDERS** like ripples in a pond."

Step 1: List your Immediate **STAKEHOLDERS** who were most affected by your decisions such as immediate family members, especially if they are having to pay court costs or are having to transport you to and from meetings with a probation officer, etc.

1. _____
2. _____
3. _____
4. _____
5. _____

Step 2: List your Important **STAKEHOLDERS** that would likely include other family members, friends, coaches, mentors, etc. who also would be affected by your good and bad decisions.

1. _____
2. _____
3. _____
4. _____
5. _____

Step 3: List your Other **STAKEHOLDERS** that would include anyone else affected like specific community members, probation officers, police, judges, bosses, school officials, etc.

1. _____
2. _____
3. _____
4. _____
5. _____

PRELUDE

⌐K **10 SMOKEFREE4ME** is designed as an education, awareness and intervention program for teens that have been experimenting with tobacco. As of 2014, the Surgeon General tells us that each day, about 3,800 kids and/or teens smoked their first cigarette. In addition to that number, 2,100 young people transform into daily cigarette smokers. Tobacco in all forms is known to be addictive, so we know that once they start smoking and/or using smokeless tobacco, these youth are not likely to quit on their own. (http://www.cdc.gov/tobacco/data_statistics/fact_sheets/youth_data/tobacco_use/, 2015)

Needless to say, this group session will not be a magic wand. The good news is that most kids are smarter than ever and smoking numbers are down. However, in 2014, nearly 4 percent of 8th graders, nearly 7.2 percent of 10th graders and nearly 13.6 percent of 12th graders had smoked a cigarette in the past 30 days and that is still far too many. (http://www.drugabuse.gov/trends-statistics/monitoring-future/monitoringfuture-study-trends-in-prevalence-various-drugs, 2015)

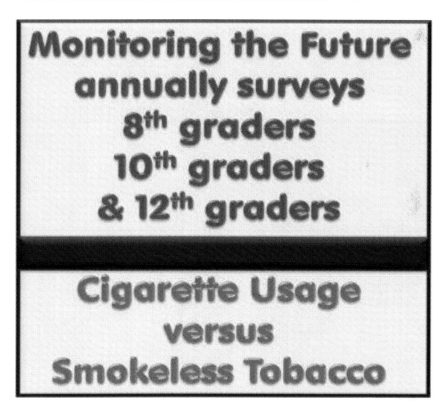

Monitoring the Future annually surveys 8th graders 10th graders & 12th graders

Cigarette Usage versus Smokeless Tobacco

Lifetime Cigarette Usage between 2012 & 2014

Every year, Monitoring the Future surveys 8th, 10th, and 12th graders. As of 2012, 2013, or 2014, the following percentage of 8th graders, 10th graders, and 12th graders have smoked a cigarette at least once.

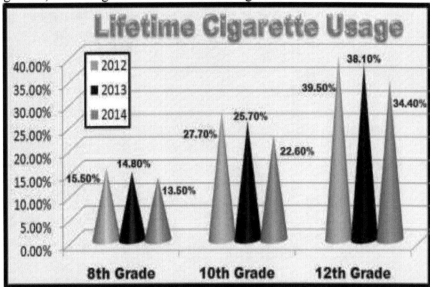

Lifetime Smokeless Tobacco Usage between 2012 & 2014

As of 2012, 2013, or 2014, the following percentage of 8th graders, 10th graders, and 12th graders have tried smokeless tobacco at least once.

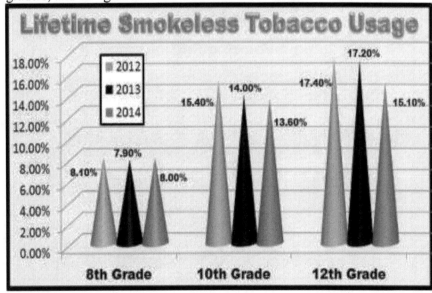

Cigarette Usage in the past month between 2012 & 2014

In 2012 to 2014, the following percentage of 8th graders, 10th graders, and 12th graders have smoked a cigarette in the past month.

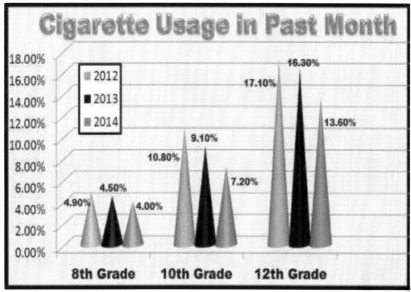

Smokeless Tobacco Usage in past month between 2012 & 2014

In 2012 to 2014, the following percentage of 8th graders, 10th graders, and 12th graders have used smokeless tobacco in past month.

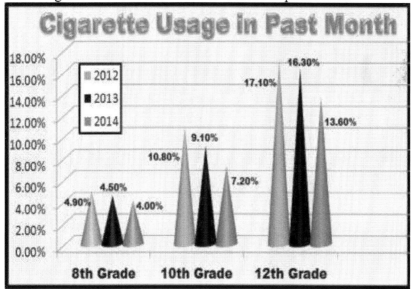

Daily Cigarette Usage in 2012 and 2014

In 2012 to 2014, the following percentage of 8th graders, 10th graders, and 12th graders smoked a cigarette daily.

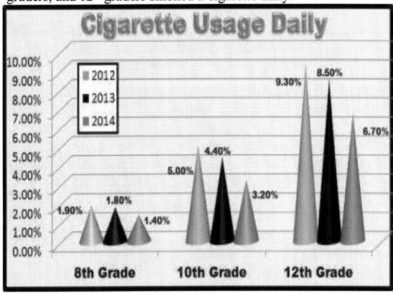

Daily Smokeless Tobacco Usage in 2012 and 2014

In 2012 to 2014, the following percentage of 8th graders, 10th graders, and 12th graders used smokeless tobacco daily.

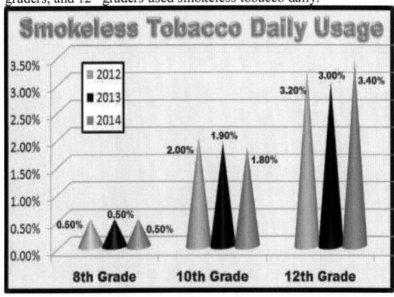

Daily Half-A-Pack Cigarette Usage in 2012 and 2014

In 2012 to 2014, the following percentage of 8th graders, 10th graders, and 12th graders smoked at least a half of a pack of cigarettes every single day.

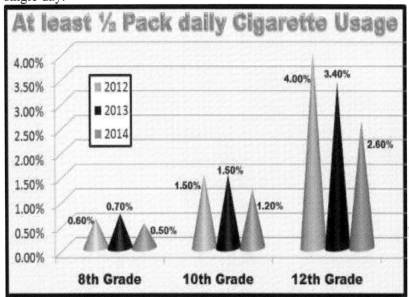

How would you respond to this Survey?

Have you ever smoked a cigarette in your life? ☐ Yes OR ☐ No

Have you smoked a cigarette in the past month? ☐ Yes OR ☐ No

Do you smoke at least one cigarette daily? ☐ Yes OR ☐ No

Do you smoke at least one-half a pack a day? ☐ Yes OR ☐ No

Have you ever used smokeless tobacco? ☐ Yes OR ☐ No

Have you used smokeless tobacco in the past month? ☐ Yes OR ☐ No

Do you use smokeless tobacco every day? ☐ Yes OR ☐ No

In our three-hour session, we will educate teens about the health risks, the woes of addiction to nicotine, and methods to combat the addiction using a renowned therapeutic method called Cognitive Behavioral Therapy (**CBT**) and Rational Emotive Behavioral Therapy (**REBT**) or what we call Rational and Logical Thinking. We also utilize other tools such as **CHARACTER COUNTS!**®[1] **The Six Pillars of Character**® while we try to empower youth to be positive and responsible people.

T = Trustworthiness
R = Respect
R = Responsibility
F = Fairness
C = Caring
C = Citizenship

This class session will be a unique experience, because each discussion will be driven by the individual participants and their personal concerns and experiences. Participants will come to successfully understand and learn from their MK 10 experience because their comments and the resulting discussions are guided through the use of "true facilitation" and utilization of the basic terminology and theories that ground **R.E.B.T.**

Dr. Albert Ellis' Cognitive and Rational Emotive Behavior Therapies **(CBT & REBT)** along with ethical-decision making skills provide the foundation for the MK 10 Program. When used properly, **CBT** and **REBT** will teach participants to dispute and uproot their own dysfunctional beliefs and take charge of their lives, thus promoting profound philosophic, emotive, and behavioral changes. However, **CBT** and **REBT** are not silver bullets.

The youth who participate in this program will have to conclude for themselves that smoking is a bad choice—pure and simple. We will give them the tools they need to think clearly and rationally for themselves, but they are the ones who will have to find the courage within to make the decision to do whatever it takes to give up the habit. It will not be easy, but nothing worth achieving usually is.

---

[1] CHARACTER COUNTS! ® and The Six Pillars of Character® are registered trademarks of the Josephson Institute. www.CharacterCounts.org

"Cigarettes are the only legal products which when used as intended – KILLS!"

-Author Unknown

Logical Thinking and Self-Control

Collective Group Activity: Introductions/Testimonial—
Out with the Old…In with the New

Participants will write the answers to the following two questions. Alternatively, you can answer the first question on one color note paper and the second question on a different color note paper.

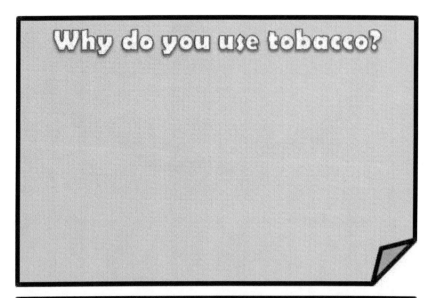

When finished, each participant will fold their responses and drop it into a box with all the other responses from the group. The facilitator will thoroughly mix the responses. Each participant will blindly draw a response from the box and read it aloud. After each response is read, its owner will retrieve it, give some thought to the responses which include **"having to, needing to, got to, must have"**, etc., wad it up, and then toss it into the wastebasket sitting in the middle of the room.

2 Tobacco questions

❶ Why do you use tobacco?

❷ What happens to you when you don't use tobacco?

Why trash it?

Because we are beginning the process of getting rid of **"Illogical Thinking"** and **"Mind Twists"** — NOW!

How do you feel about Tobacco?

Individual Activity: Take a few minutes to fill in how you feel about the following questions. Then we'll move on to discuss this later in session.

How do you feel about Tobacco?	Agree	Disagree
I would prefer to date people who don't smoke.		
Smoking is a dirty habit.		
I think that becoming a smoker reflects poor judgment.		
I strongly dislike being near people who are smoking.		
I personally don't mind being around people who are smoking.		
The harmful effects of cigarettes have been exaggerated.		
Smokers know how to enjoy life more than nonsmokers.		

The Smoking Survey-How Do You Compare to the Nation?

Collective Group Discussion: How do you compare to the nation?

According to the National Center for Chronic Disease Prevention and Health Promotion and the Tobacco Information and Prevention Source (TIPS), at
http://www.cdc.gov/tobacco/tips_4_youth/facts.htm
(2005 to 2009),

See this page and the next page to see what teens across the USA said in response to these statements about tobacco usage. Please note that these percentages have not been updated since 2009. In fact, you have to check some archive sections on the internet to find these results listed currently. Please also note that e-cigarettes were not included in the former survey. That was added in by the **MK** editor.   Archive listing:
http://web.archive.org/web/20041016002839/http://www.cdc.go
v/tobacco/tips_4_youth/facts.htm (found 2015)

How do you compare to the following survey questions?

How do you feel about tobacco?	Agree	Disagree	No Opinion or Don't Know
The Answers were Compiled in 2009.			
Seeing someone smoke turns me off.	67%	22%	10%
I'd rather date people who don't smoke.	86%	8%	6%
It's safe to smoke for only a year or two.	7%	92%	1%
Smoking can help when you're bored.	7%	92%	1%

How do you feel about tobacco?	Agree	Disagree	No Opinion or Don't Know
Smoking helps reduce stress.	21%	78%	3%
Smoking helps keep your weight down.	18%	80%	2%
Chewing tobacco and snuff causes cancer.	95%	2%	3%
I strongly dislike being around smokers.	65%	22%	13%

How did you compare to this survey question? How do you think other teens in the nation would respond to this question?

As of 2015, more Current Answers Have Not Been Yet Been Compiled.			
E-Cigarettes are much safer than cigarettes.	?	?	?

Some Thought-Provoking Facts

Updated October 1, 2015, here are some thought-provoking facts:
(http://www.cdc.gov/tobacco/data_statistics/fact_sheets/health_effe
cts/effects_cig_smoking/)

◯ More than 10 times as many U.S. citizens have died prematurely from cigarette smoking than have died in all the wars fought by the United States during its history.

◯ Smoking can cause cancer almost anywhere in your body.

◯ If nobody smoked, one of every three cancer deaths in the United States would not happen.

◯ Smoking harms nearly every organ of the body and affects a person's overall health.

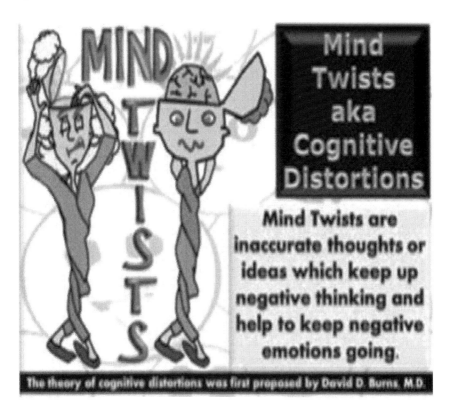

Dr. Albert Ellis, the father of **R.E.B.T.** which stands for **R**ational **E**motive **B**ehavioral Therapy, focuses on the use of the following terms that are known as "Cognitive Distortions" or "Mind Twists":

- **Awfulizing**
- **Musts**
- **Shoulds**
- **Have to's**
- **and being "Should on"**

Why do you think he focuses on the use of these words?

The theory of cognitive distortions was first proposed by David D. Burns, M.D. [2]

A-B-C-D-E-F & S H's of R.E.B.T. (Rational Emotive Behavioral Therapy) and Mind Twists

We are going to explore one of the most profound methods for bringing about a positive KEY mindset of rational and emotional change.

The sophisticated name for it is **R.E.B.T.** which stands for **R**ational **E**motive **B**ehavioral **T**herapy. We'll just call it LOGICAL THINKING. This type of thinking helps us get rid of a LOCKED mindset of irrational, illogical beliefs that some people call "Stinking Thinking."

[2] Burns, David D., MD. 1989. The Feeling Good Handbook. New York: William Morrow and Company, Inc.

3 examples of STINKING THINKING vs. LOGICAL THINKING:

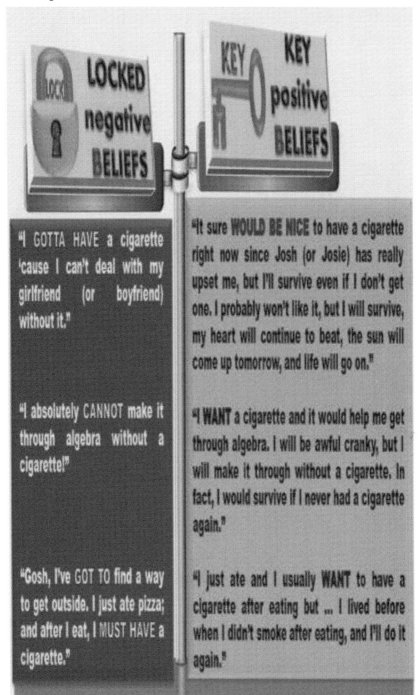

LOCKED negative BELIEFS

KEY positive BELIEFS

"I GOTTA HAVE a cigarette 'cause I can't deal with my girlfriend (or boyfriend) without it."

"It sure WOULD BE NICE to have a cigarette right now since Josh (or Josie) has really upset me, but I'll survive even if I don't get one. I probably won't like it, but I will survive, my heart will continue to beat, the sun will come up tomorrow, and life will go on."

"I absolutely CANNOT make it through algebra without a cigarette!"

"I WANT a cigarette and it would help me get through algebra. I will be awful cranky, but I will make it through without a cigarette. In fact, I would survive if I never had a cigarette again."

"Gosh, I've GOT TO find a way to get outside. I just ate pizza; and after I eat, I MUST HAVE a cigarette."

"I just ate and I usually WANT to have a cigarette after eating but ... I lived before when I didn't smoke after eating, and I'll do it again."

A volunteer will read the following statement:

"Illogical Thinking" does not accurately reflect reality. To survive life's greatest difficulties, we must learn to see life clearly.

We need to realize that although we may not be able to control everything that happens outside of us, we can control how we react, what we think, feel, do, and say.

No one can force us to believe things we don't want to believe, or behave in ways we don't want to behave, unless we give them control over us. We have so much —too much— to live for. Only we can make and stick to the decision to keep control over ourselves.

We need to begin to realize that everything we do *begins in our thought processes*. In other words, our actions don't become our actions until we think about it. Located in some place in our mind — our thoughts become beliefs. Then, we begin to act on our beliefs.

This is what we are looking at in this session. **R.E.B.T.** or "**Logical Thinking**" is a part of the cognitive behavioral approach. Cognitive basically means relating to thought processes.

One thing we want to do from the very beginning is to learn to quit making excuses, quit blaming others and other situations for our problems. Most of all, *get rid of negative, stinking thinking by starting to think logically*.

Please note: Here is the overview of the next several pages:

A-B-C-D-E-F and 8 H's of R.E.B.T.

Activating Event

Heat of the Moment

Head - Thoughts

Heart - Emotions

Beliefs about Events

Hunch – Trust your Gut

Consequences

Hands – Action Taken

Debate Negative Unhelpful Beliefs

Haggle – Hash Out

Habit – Habitual (Default) Responses to Stressors

Effective New Beliefs

Functional Emotions, Behaviors, & Health

Healthy & Whole

The Effects of Tobacco on Sean Marsee and Other Teens

♦ See MK1-MK10 Facilitator's Manual pp. 177-180

Sean Marsee (1965-1984). Photo credit: SeanMarsee.jpg.
Creative Commons, Attribution-ShareAlike 30.0 Unported (CC BY-SA 3.0)

What does Lung Cancer and Joyriding have in Common?

Lung Cancer vs. Joyriding

♦ See MK1-MK10
Facilitator's Manual
pp. 187-190

"Lack of willpower
has caused more
failure than
lack of intelligence
or ability."
--Florence A. Newhouse

Collaborative Group Activity:

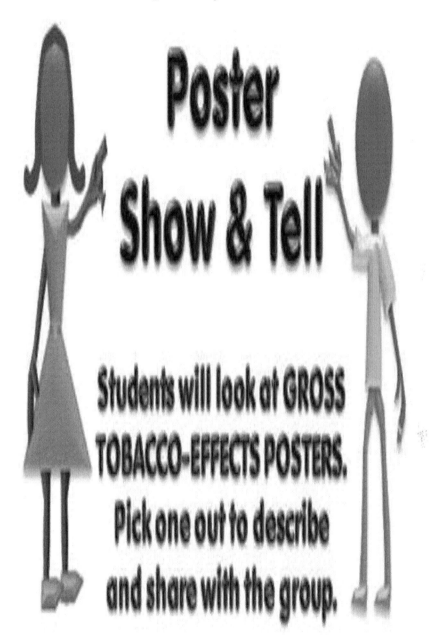

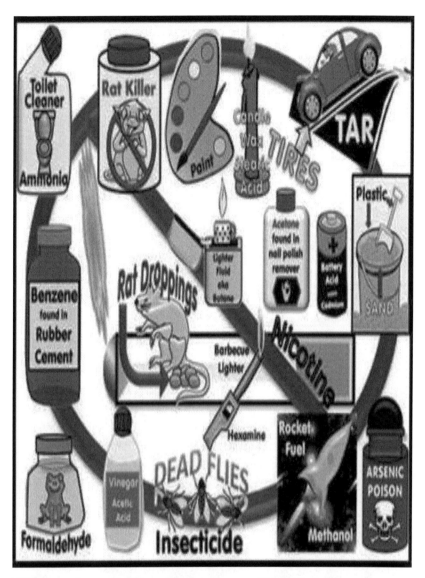

7000 chemicals including Toilet Cleaner – Ammonia, Rat Killer, Paint, Candle Wax – Stearic Acid, Tires, Tar, Benzene found in Rubber Cement, Rat Droppings, Lighter Fluid aka Butane, Acetone found in Nail Polish Remover, Battery Acid – Cadmium, Plastic, Sand, Barbecue Lighter – Hexamine, Nicotine, Formaldehyde, Vinegar – Acetic Acid, Dead Flies, Insecticide, Rocket Fuel – Methanol, & Arsenic Poison.

Collaborative Group Activity:

Which thumb is on top?

Clasp your hands together with your fingers intertwined.

❖   Which thumb is on top?

Now switch your hands so the other thumb is on top.

❖   How does it feel?

❖   How hard did you have to think about it?

❖   What do you think you would have to do for that to feel comfortable?

Once something is a habit and it feels comfortable, it is very difficult to change — but it is possible — especially when we have a strategy to practice doing it a different way.

Collaborative Group Activity:

Folding Arms & Habit-Breaking

Fold your arms across your waist.

❖ Which arm is on top?

Now try folding your arms with the other arm on top.

❖ How does it feel?

❖ How hard did you have to think about it?

❖ What do you think you would have to do for that to feel comfortable?

Just like when you did this with your thumbs, you do it the same way –automatically, without thinking about it. The way that you learned to do this has become a habit and it feels comfortable.

How old were you when you first began using Tobacco???

Narrator ❶: Let's talk about each of you. Think back to the very first time you ever smoked, dipped, or chewed any kind of tobacco product.

A of the A-B-C-D-E-F of H.E.B.H

H-1 Heat of the Moment

A Activating Event

Narrator ❷: Tell about that very first ACTIVATING HEAT-OF-THE-MOMENT EVENT.

1 How old were you?

_____

2 Who was involved?

_____

3 Where did this event take place

_____

4 How did it happen?

_____

Narrator ❶: Tell what your HEAD was thinking and your HEART was feeling. Verbally fill in the blanks.

H-2 Head •Thoughts

H-3 Heart •Emotions

5 My HEAD was thinking:

_____
_____
_____

6 My HEART was feeling:

_____
_____
_____

Narrator ②: What was your BELIEF or HUNCH about the wisdom of agreeing to try out either ALCOHOL or DRUGS or both? Did you think it was a good idea, scary idea, bad idea, or some other kind of idea?

⑦ My BELIEF or HUNCH was:

_____

_____

_____

Narrator ①: What was the CONSEQUENCE of this event? What Action did your HANDS take, so to speak?

⑧ The action my HANDS took was

_____

_____

_____

Narrator ②: Did you DEBATE and HAGGLE about the wisdom of making this less-than-wise ALCOHOL-or-DRUG-using choice, or did you decide to do this right away? Why or why not?

⑨ Did you try to say 'No' or did you say 'Yes' right away? Why or why not?

_____

_____

_____

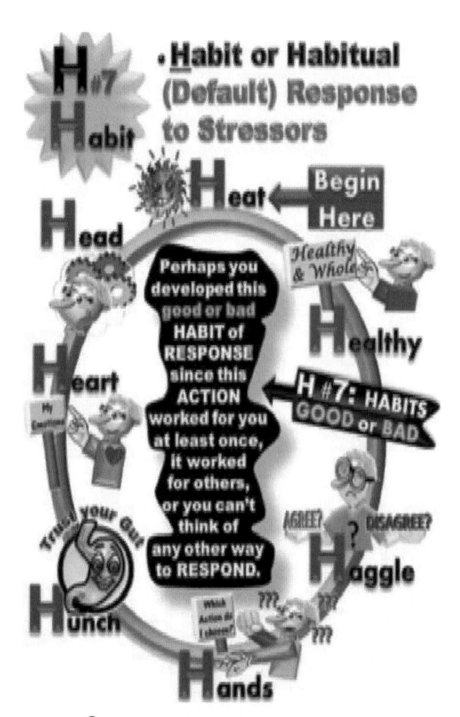

Habit or Habitual (Default) Response to Stressors

H #7 / Habit

Begin Here

Heat

Head

Healthy & Whole

Healthy

Perhaps you developed this good or bad HABIT of RESPONSE since this ACTION worked for you at least once, it worked for others, or you can't think of any other way to RESPOND.

H #7: HABITS GOOD or BAD

Heart

My Emotions

Trust your Gut

AGREE? ? DISAGREE?

Haggle

Hunch

Which Action do I choose?

Hands

Narrator ❶: How long did it take before this type of ALC0HOL-or-DRUG-using choice became a HABIT for you?

⑩ It took _____ hours, days, weeks, months, or years before this type of ALCOHOL-or-DRUG-using choice became a HABIT because

_____

_____

_____

Narrator ❶: What are your concerns or thoughts about whether you will remain HEALTHY and Whole in spite of making this type of ALCOHOL-or-DRUG-using choice?

_____

_____

_____

⑪ Do I have concerns about my physical and/or emotional HEALTH regarding making this type of ALCOHOL-or-DRUG-using choice(s)? Why or why not?

_____

_____

_____

⑫ If I do have physical and/or emotional HEALTH concerns, what are they? Please explain.

_____

_____

_____

Listed below are some examples of cognitive distortions. Perhaps you will recognize some of these as struggles for yourself or for other people I know. There are ten main Mind Twists / BELIEFS for us to consider. Give examples in the space provided.

LIST OF 10 COGNITIVE DISTORTIONS	All-or-Nothing Thinking	Overgeneralization
	MIND TWIST #1	MIND TWIST #2
Mental Filter & Disqualifying the Positive	Jumping to Conclusions, Mind Reading, & The Fortune Teller Error	Magnification, Minimization, Catastrophizing, & Awfulizing
MIND TWIST #3	MIND TWIST #4	MIND TWIST #5
Should, Must, & Have To	Labeling & Mislabeling	Emotional Reasoning, Personalization, & Blaming
MIND TWIST #6	MIND TWIST #7	MIND TWIST #8
Always Being Right	Fallacies of Control, Fairness, & Change plus Magical Thinking	Which ones challenges you the most?
MIND TWIST #9	MIND TWIST #10	

Mind Twist/Cognitive Distortion #1 of 10: All-or-Nothing Thinking:

TASK: By looking at the picture, interpret what you think this particular Mind Twist/Cognitive Distortion means.

Regarding violating this law, write in some possible All-Or-Nothing Thinking you've employed in the middle column and some more balanced BELIEFS in the right-hand column.

MIND TWISTS	LOCKED negative BELIEFS	KEY positive BELIEFS
Using tobacco products		

Mind Twist/Cognitive Distortion #2 of 10: Overgeneralization

TASK: By looking at the picture, interpret what you think this particular Mind Twist/Cognitive Distortion means.

MIND TWISTS	LOCKED negative BELIEFS	KEY positive BELIEFS
Using tobacco products		

 Page 38

Mind Twist/Cognitive Distortion #3 of 10: Mental Filter & Disqualifying the Positive

TASK: By looking at the picture, interpret what you think this particular Mind Twist/Cognitive Distortion means.

MIND TWISTS	LOCKED negative BELIEFS	KEY positive BELIEFS
Using tobacco products		

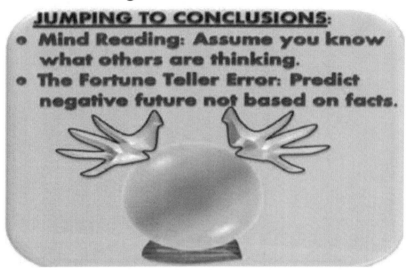

JUMPING TO CONCLUSIONS:
- **Mind Reading: Assume you know what others are thinking.**
- **The Fortune Teller Error: Predict negative future not based on facts.**

TASK: By looking at the picture, interpret what you think this particular Mind Twist/Cognitive Distortion means.

MIND TWISTS	LOCKED negative BELIEFS	KEY positive BELIEFS
Using tobacco products		

Mind Twist/Cognitive Distortion #5 of 10: Magnification, Minimization, Catastrophizing, & Awfulizing

MAGNIFICATION / MINIMIZATION / CATASTROPHIZING / AWFULIZING:
- Exaggerate or Minimize importance of events.
- Seeing only awful outcomes plus visualizing catastrophes.

TASK: By looking at the picture, interpret what you think this particular Mind Twist/Cognitive Distortion means.

MIND TWISTS	LOCKED negative BELIEFS	KEY positive BELIEFS
Using tobacco products		

Mind Twist/Cognitive Distortion #6 of 10: Should, Must, and Have To

SHOULD, MUST, & HAVE TO STATEMENTS:
- **When you direct "SHOULD" statements toward yourself or others, you feel anger, frustration, resentment, or guilt.**

SHOULD

Stop SHOULDing me!

TASK: By looking at the picture, interpret what you think this particular Mind Twist/Cognitive Distortion means. Mind Twist / Cognitive Distortion #7 of 10: Labeling and Mislabeling

MIND TWISTS	LOCKED negative BELIEFS	KEY positive BELIEFS
Using tobacco products		

LABELING & MISLABELING:

o Put Down Self, Others, or Life in General.

I'm such a loser.

He (or She) is such a jerk.

Life is the pits.

TASK: By looking at the picture, interpret what you think this particular Mind Twist/Cognitive Distortion means.

MIND TWISTS	LOCKED negative BELIEFS	KEY positive BELIEFS
Using tobacco products		

EMOTIONAL REASONING: • I feel like a bad person; therefore, I must be a bad person.
• I feel it; therefore, it must be true.

PERSONALIZATION & BLAMING:

• My parents divorced; therefore, it must be my fault. **VERSUS**

• I broke curfew and got grounded. It's all my friend's fault for talking me into doing this.

• We blame ourselves for something even though it was not really our fault. **VERSUS**

• Even though our attitude and behavior might have contributed to a problem, we blame others.

Here's the picture again:

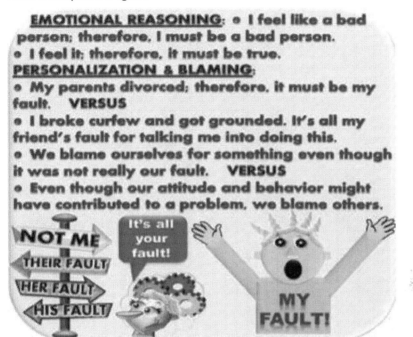

EMOTIONAL REASONING: • I feel like a bad person; therefore, I must be a bad person.
• I feel it; therefore, it must be true.
PERSONALIZATION & BLAMING:
• My parents divorced; therefore, it must be my fault. VERSUS
• I broke curfew and got grounded. It's all my friend's fault for talking me into doing this.
• We blame ourselves for something even though it was not really our fault. VERSUS
• Even though our attitude and behavior might have contributed to a problem, we blame others.

NOT ME
THEIR FAULT
HER FAULT
HIS FAULT
It's all your fault!
MY FAULT!

TASK: By looking at the picture, interpret what you think this particular Mind Twist/Cognitive Distortion means.

MIND TWISTS	LOCKED negative BELIEFS	KEY positive BELIEFS
Using tobacco products		

ALWAYS BEING RIGHT:

- I am convinced I am always right. I am determined to convince you of this as well.
- Being wrong is unthinkable.
- My being right is more important than how you feel or think.

Can't you admit you were wrong this time?

I am NEVER wrong! I am ALWAYS right!

Here's the picture again:

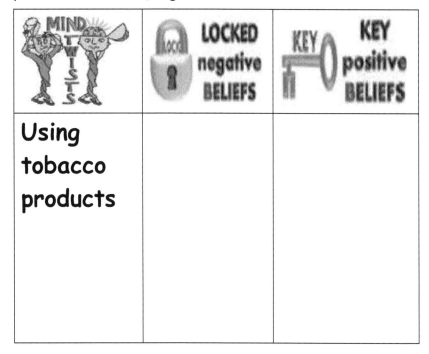

ALWAYS BEING RIGHT:
- I am convinced I am always right. I am determined to convince you of this as well.
- Being wrong is unthinkable.
- My being right is more important than how you feel or think.

Can't you admit you were wrong this time?

I am NEVER wrong! I am ALWAYS right!

TASK: By looking at the picture, interpret what you think this particular Mind Twist/Cognitive Distortion means.

MIND TWISTS	LOCKED negative BELIEFS	KEY positive BELIEFS
Using tobacco products		

FALLACIES OF CONTROL:

- If we feel externally controlled, we see ourselves as a helpless victim of fate.
- If we are internally controlled, we assume responsibility for the pain and happiness of everyone around you.

FALLACIES OF FAIRNESS:

- We resent it that LIFE is not always fair. This goes against our expectations and desires.

FALLACIES OF CHANGE:

- We expect others to change to suit us if we simply apply enough nagging and pressure.

MAGICAL THINKING:

- The belief that acts will influence unrelated situations. We expect our sacrifice and self-denial to pay off, as if someone is keeping score.

I am a good person, so bad things should not happen to me.

Here's the picture again:

FALLACIES OF CONTROL:
• If we feel externally controlled, we see ourselves as a helpless victim of fate.
• If we are internally controlled, we assume responsibility for the pain and happiness of everyone around you.
FALLACIES OF FAIRNESS:
• We resent it that LIFE is not always fair. This goes against our expectations and desires.
FALLACIES OF CHANGE:
• We expect others to change to suit us if we simply apply enough nagging and pressure.

Life is NOT fair!

Fairness Meter

MAGICAL THINKING:
• The belief that acts will influence unrelated situations. We expect our sacrifice and self-denial to pay off, as if someone is keeping score.

Magical Thinking

I am a good person, so bad things should not happen to me.

TASK: By looking at the picture, interpret what you think this particular Mind Twist/Cognitive Distortion means.

MIND TWISTS	LOCKED negative BELIEFS	KEY positive BELIEFS
Using tobacco products		

Head, Heart, & Hand Balloon Game

Step 1:
Blow up Balloon.

Then, write Irrational, Illogical Belief Statement on Balloon.

Examples

I can't make it through math class without sneaking some dip.

Step 2:
Get in circle.

Launch balloon off your head.

This symbolizes how all your thoughts and Logical and Illogical beliefs begins in your head.

Step 3:
Attempt to keep the balloon in the air using your head, your hands, and your chest.

If your balloon hits the ground or pops, sit out the rest of the game.

Hitting the balloon with your chest ...

... symbolizes how your thoughts trickle to your heart, which begins to change how you feel inside.

Hitting the balloon with your hands ...

... symbolizes how your thoughts and feelings turned into action.

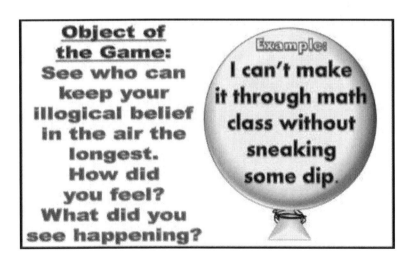

Object of the Game: See who can keep your illogical belief in the air the longest. How did you feel? What did you see happening?

Example: I can't make it through math class without sneaking some dip.

Directions for Quiz Bowl

1 Each participant will write their answers to the questions for points. If answered correctly, they will get 100 points per question. Once all the 100-point questions are asked, they will post their total points below.

2 Each participant will answer the questions for 200 points per question. If answered correctly, they will get 200 points per question. Once all the 200-point questions are asked, they will post their total points below.

3 Participants will repeat the same for 300-point questions.

4 Each participant will add their total cumulative points from all point categories.

5 Participants may choose to wager all or part of their points.

6 At the end, the participant with the highest points wins a gift.

100 Points Total =	
200 Points Total =	
300 Points Total =	
Total Cumulative Score =	
Total Amount Wagered =	
Total Score After Wager =	

MK QUIZ BOWL

100 pts	200 pts	300 pts
Q #1	Q #1	Q #1
Q #2	Q #2	Q #2
Q #3	Q #3	Q #3
Q #4	Q #4	Q #4
Q #5	Q #5	Q #5

Answer Key in Facilitator's Manual pp. 376-385

MK Quiz Bowl Questions

Circle Your Answers

Questions worth 100 Points

1 TRUE or FALSE	The number of teens who smoke is going up.
2 TRUE or FALSE	More Americans die from cigarette-related illnesses than alcohol, car accidents, suicide, AIDS, homicide and illegal drugs combined.
3 TRUE or FALSE	Symptoms of addiction such as having strong urges to smoke, feeling anxious or irritable, or having unsuccessfully tried not to smoke can appear in teens and preteens within weeks or only days after they become "occasional" smokers.
4 TRUE or FALSE	Teens and preteens who smoke are more susceptible to colds as those who don't smoke.
5 TRUE or FALSE	Almost 2 of 10 lung cancer deaths are caused by smoking cigarettes.

Questions worth 200 Points

1 MORE or LESS	Cigarettes kill 1,000 Americans every day.
2 TRUE or FALSE	On average, smokers die 10 years earlier than nonsmokers.
3 TRUE or FALSE	From 2013 to 2014, E-cigarette use triples among middle and high school students in just one year.
4 TRUE or FALSE	Vaping is a totally safe alternative to smoking cigarettes.
5 TRUE or FALSE	Using "chewing" or "smokeless" tobacco is as dangerous as smoking cigarettes.

Questions worth 300 Points

❶ **TRUE or FALSE**	General's Report issued in May, 2004, smoking is even worse than previously thought. It damages virtually every organ in the body.
❷ **Circle one:** **10 seconds** **25 seconds** **60 seconds**	After a puff of a cigarette, nicotine is in the brain in how many seconds?
❸ **TRUE or FALSE**	Smoking suppresses the appetite.
❹ **TRUE or FALSE**	Tobacco use is started and established primarily during adolescence.
❺ **TRUE or FALSE**	Cigarette companies look to young people as replacement smokers.

Wager Question

Name two drugs that are as addictive as nicotine.

Nicotine is as addictive as

_____ and _____.

Self-Control and Willpower Quiz

❶ I control how I react to situations, events in life, and how I react to others.	☐ YES ☐ NO
❷ I control who I let into my life and who I decide to spend my time with.	☐ YES ☐ NO
❸ I control my actions.	☐ YES ☐ NO
❹ I I control my thoughts.	☐ YES ☐ NO
❺ I control my positive or negative self-talk.	☐ YES ☐ NO
❻ I control the positive or negative relationships I'm in.	☐ YES ☐ NO
❼ I control what I eat or don't eat.	☐ YES ☐ NO
❽ I control my outlook about the future.	☐ YES ☐ NO
❾ I control whether or not I set goals.	☐ YES ☐ NO
❿ I determine my attitude.	☐ YES ☐ NO
⓫ I control if I decide to be open-minded or close-minded to new ideas and opportunities.	☐ YES ☐ NO
⓬ I control whether or not I use tobacco products.	☐ YES ☐ NO

Responsibility

Now that we've worked through the quiz, let's review the definitions of **RESPONSIBILITY** from the last session and let's answer the following three questions:

❶ Who really has the **RESPONSIBILITY** for controlling your behavior?

❷ Although there are, and always will be things beyond your control, who has the RESPONSIBILITY and power to control how you prepare for and react to them?

❸ For every decision you make, is there a direct result or consequence? What is the term for those who are affected by your decisions?

Collective Discussion: Group will discuss this quote:

"When you decide your life is your own, it becomes so. No excuses, no one to rely on, no one to blame. You can't control all your circumstances, but you can control your reactions and what you learn."

--Michael Josephson, Founder of CHARACTER COUNTS!

Individual Activity: On another sheet of paper or in the box below, draw a picture, write a poem, or create a song (or a parody by changing words to an existing song) that illustrates what being in control of yourself means to you:

Some definitions of self-control follow:

Self-control is the ability to control one's emotions, behavior and desires in order to obtain some reward later. Self-regulation. (http://virtuefirst.org/virtues/self-control/)

Self-denial: the act of denying yourself; controlling your impulses (http://www.vocabulary.com/dictionary/self-denial)

Does your definition come close to these two? What about your drawing, song or poem? Does it represent the definitions above in any way?

Read this statement:

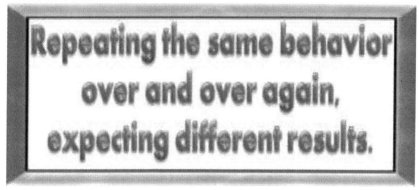

Repeating the same behavior over and over again, expecting different results.

What would you call that process?

Some people say that it is the definition of **insanity**.

Collective Group Discussion: What do you think that definition of insanity means specifically?

How does it apply to your lives?

Self-Control and Tobacco

It is important to realize that having enough will power and self-control may not be enough when it comes to addiction to tobacco.

As you will learn, if you don't know already, the tobacco industry and the media have spent a lot of time and money to make you purchase and become addicted to their products.

Self-control is very important in your journey toward a successful life, but please know that you may need additional help to truly stop using tobacco. Tobacco is more addictive than alcohol plus some of the most addictive drugs like cocaine and heroin and really hard to stop once you're addicted—which doesn't take very long.

If you need it, don't be afraid to ASK FOR HELP!

Always remember that those who are most successful in life are not afraid to ask for and get the help they need. The weak person is the very one who refuses to get help; and more than likely, that person will fail in the long-run. You may need to seek the help of a medical doctor, a psychologist or perhaps a parent/caregiver or other mentor who will help you find the assistance you need.

Whatever your situation, be the strong and successful person you want to be and ask for and get the help you need to make positive changes in your life! Ten years from now, you'll be so glad you did.

Peer pressure is, indeed, a huge reason why many teens start and even continue to use tobacco. You will clearly see later on, the majority of teens choose not to use tobacco. Using tobacco is no longer the norm. In fact, in the years to come, tobacco may very well be a part of the past because logical people are beginning to realize the benefits of not using tobacco products EVER!

We've all heard about the **"Just Say No"** campaign, and perhaps you may have thought it was cheesy. **Well, is it cheesy to be an assertive person who is proud of standing up for your beliefs?**

It is really empowering when you stand up to someone who's trying to pressure you to do something you really don't want to do and you simply tell them, **"No thanks, that's really not for me."** When you walk away, you feel like you are in control of your life. That's self-control at its best.

Collective Group Discussion: Participants share specifically how they've stood up to peer pressure and how they've said "No" to tobacco, drugs or alcohol and been able to successfully walk away.

Collective Discussion: Group will discuss these quotes:

> "Keep away from people who try to belittle your situations. Small people always do that, but the really great make you feel that you, too, can become great."
> --Mark Twain

> "Whether you think you can or you think you can't, you're right."
> --Henry Ford

> "Nothing is impossible, the word itself says 'I'm possible'!"
> --Audrey Hepburn

impossible ➔ I'm possible

> "Do or do not. There is no try."
> --Yoda

Self-Control and Saying "NO!"

Collective Group Activity:

1 Participants will stand and each will be given a wooden clothespin.

2 Each will use their non-prominent hand to hold onto the clothespin with just the tips of their thumb and first finger (index finger). They are to hold the clothespin straight out from their fingers (As they are holding the clothespin, they cannot use any other part of their body or fingers to help hold onto it).

3 The facilitator will start time and each participant will try to see how many times they can open and close the clothespin within 60 seconds. Each will share their number with the group.

4 Next each participant will hold the clothespin open and they will be timed to see how long they can hold it open. The facilitator will call out the time in 15 second increments.

5 As each participant finds they can no longer hold their clothespin open, they should sit down.

6 The group will continue until the last person sits down.

7 Ask them to reflect on the experience.

a)   How did it feel to open/close?

b)   Was it easier to keep it going or holding it open the entire time?

c)   How did it feel to keep it open?

d) Did everyone sit down at the same time?

e) Did you want to "WIN"? Did the desire to win keep you going even when you were in pain?

f) How could this activity apply to peer pressure?

(Hint: Opening and closing is like getting into situations where people are making poor decisions and then removing yourself – it is not as painful as being in the situation and then pulling yourself out. While being in situations where you are with people making poor choices is more painful, some people will give in and reduce the pain more quickly while others will continue to be propelled by the competition or the peer pressure even though they are in pain.)

g) How does this activity apply to self-control with tobacco use? '

(Adapted from Tom Jackson's "Activities that Teach")

Collective Discussion: Group will discuss this quote:

"Stand up for what is right, Even if you are standing alone."

-- Author Unknown

How Much Is It Costing You?

According to research, most teens spend about $1,000 per year on tobacco products. However, below is a formula to help you decide according to your own habit.

Cigarette Costs by State

Average price of a pack of cigarettes for 2014, from least to most expensive:

http://www.fool.com/investing/general/2014/09/27/the-surprising-cost-of-a-pack-a-day-in-all-50stat.aspx, 2015

#	State	Avg. price per Pack	Cost over 1 yr	Cost over 20 yrs
1	Virginia	$5.25	$1,916	$38,325
2	Missouri	$5.25	$1,916	$38,325
3	Tennessee	$5.30	$1,935	$38,690
4	North Dakota	$5.33	$1,945	$38,909
5	Kentucky	$5.40	$1,971	$38,420
6	Wyoming	$5.41	$1,975	$39,493
7	Idaho	$5.41	$1,975	$39, 493
8	West Virginia	$5.43	$1,982	$39.639
9	Louisiana	$5.44	$1,986	$39,712
10	North Carolina	$5.45	$1,989	$39,785
11	Alabama	$5.51	$2,011	$40,223
12	South Carolina	$5.58	$2,037	$40,734
13	Colorado	$5.65	$2,062	$41.245
14	Oregon	$5.69	$2,077	$41,537
15	Kansas	$5.83	$2,128	$42,537
16	California	$5.89	$2,150	$42,997
17	Indiana	$5.97	$2,179	$43,581
18	Ohio	$6.03	$2,201	$44,019
19	Arkansas	$6.07	$2,216	$44,311
20	South Dakota	$6.08	$2,219	$44,384
21	Nevada	$6.15	$2,245	$44,895
22	Nebraska	$6.23	$2,274	$45,479
23	Oklahoma	$6.29	$2,296	$45,917
24	Iowa	$6.29	$2,296	$45,917
25	Florida	$6.30	$2,300	$45,990

#	State	Avg. price per Pack	Cost over 1 yr	Cost over 20 yrs
26	Mississippi	$6.34	$2,314	$46,282
27	Delaware	$6.35	$2,318	$46,355
28	Georgia	$6.39	$2,332	$46,647
29	New Hampshire	$6.44	$2,351	$47,012
30	$6.46	$2,358	$47,158	$6.46
31	$6.69	$2,442	$48,837	$6.69
32	$6.85	$2,500	$50,005	$6.85
33	$6.89	$2,515	$50,297	$6.89
34	$7.37	$2,690	$53,801	$7.37
35	$7.67	$2,800	$55,991	$7.67
36	$7.75	$2,829	$56,575	$7.75
37	$7.99	$2,916	$58,327	$7.99
38	$8.00	$2,920	$58,400	$8.00
39	$8.05	$2,938	$58,765	$8.05
40	$8.10	$2,957	$59,130	$8.10
41	$8.20	$2,993	$59,860	$8.20
42	$8.82	$3,219	$64,386	$8.82
43	$8.95	$3,267	$65,335	$8.95
44	$9.30	$3,395	$67,890	$9.30
45	$9.52	$3,475	$69,496	$9.52
46	$9.55	$3,486	$69,715	$9.55
47	$9.62	$3,511	$70,226	$9.62
48	$9.79	$3,573	$71,467	$9.79
49	$9.95	$3,632	$72,635	$9.95
50	$11.50	$4,198	$83,950	$11.50

Smokeless Tobacco Costs by State

(The following is an estimation based on national averages)

- Cost of dipping = one can per day x 365 days x cost per can x # of years dipped

- i.e. - If you dip one half a can per day for 4 years at $5.00 per can, your habit will cost $912.50

- i.e. –If you dip two cans per day at $50.00 per ten pack roll for one year, your cost would be $3,650.00

Collaborative Group Activity: Form small groups and discuss what else you could do with $1,000 a year, more or less, and then $4,000 during the course of your high school career. Then have a collective discussion about your ideas. Write these below.

Things I could purchase with $1,000:

1._____   4._____
2._____   5._____
3._____   6._____

Things I could purchase with $4,000:

1._____   4._____
2._____   5._____
3._____   6._____

Why Did You Do It?

Collaborative Group Activity: Form small groups and *discuss why you first started smoking or why you smoked or used tobacco recently.* This list might include:

- ☐ To look cool
- ☐ To look sexy
- ☐ To relax
- ☐ My parents told me not to
- ☐ To lose weight
- ☐ To feel mature
- ☐ Everyone else was doing it
- ☐ Couldn't say no to my friends

…Then, discuss the drawbacks or negatives to smoking. What have you experienced or think might be the downside to smoking? These might include:

- ☐ Bad breath
- ☐ Yellow teeth
- ☐ Smelly clothes
- ☐ Holes in clothes
- ☐ Smelly room
- ☐ Other people's opinion of you as a tobacco user

How do you feel about having bad breath, smelly clothes, etc.?

A Breathing & Exercise Experiment

(Participants who don't feel comfortable or who have any kind of medical condition such as asthma, acute bronchitis, heart problems, etc., should abstain from participation in the following activity.)

Collective Group Activity:

❶ Participants will stand.

❷ When prompted they will begin to jog in place together. As they begin their journey, remind them to breathe deeply and to keep going. (Facilitator will describe the path— May be up and down hills, across the park, around the river, on the beach, etc. This will continue for about 2-3 minutes.

❸ Each participant will receive a drinking straw.

❹ Participants will continue their jog but now they can only breathe through the straw.

❺ NO ONE CONTINUES IF THEY FEEL FAINT OR LIGHTHEADED.

❻ The group will compare the two experiences.

❼ The group will then relate this experience to smoking.

Hint: The tar from cigarettes goes into the lungs and is trapped inside the "alveoli" (tiny sacs in the lungs). The body reacts by reducing the function of the lungs making it harder to breathe. Over time it can turn into a life-threatening condition of emphysema. The reduction of breathing capacity can happen quickly after even just a short time of smoking.

More Facts To Be Considered:

* Here is more food for thought from the Campaign for Tobacco-Free Kids…

* Smoking can also seriously harm kids while they are still young. Besides the immediate bad breath, irritated eyes and throat, and increased heartbeat and blood pressure, there are short-term harms for youth who smoke or use smokeless tobacco including respiratory problems, reduced immune function, increased illness, tooth decay, gum disease, and pre-cancerous gene mutations.

* The cigarette companies spend more than $15.4 billion each year to promote their deadly product. That's more than $42 million spent every day to market cigarettes. Much of that marketing directly reaches and influences kids.

* Kids are more susceptible to cigarette advertising and marketing than adults. While only half of smokers over age 25 buy the top three brands, 82 percent of youth smokers (ages 12 to 17) choose the three most heavily advertised brands: Marlboro, Camel, and Newport.

* A journal of the National Cancer Institute study found that teens were more likely to be influenced to smoke by cigarette marketing than by peer pressure. Similarly, a Journal of the American Medical Association study found that as much as a third of underage experimentation with smoking was attributable to tobacco company marketing efforts.

* Internal company documents revealed a definite marketing strategy for spit tobacco, targeting kids. In 1993, cherry flavoring was added to UST's SKOAL Long Cut, another starter product. A former UST sales representative revealed that, "Cherry SKOAL is for somebody who likes the taste of candy, if you know what I'm saying."

Dissect the Advertisement:

Make no doubt about it, as you can see above, the tobacco industry has lured you like luring children to candy. They've used everything from sexy men and women to candy-like persuasion, to cartoons like the infamous "Joe Camel."

Joe Camel (officially Old Joe) was the advertising mascot for Camel cigarettes from late 1987 to July 12, 1997, appearing in magazine advertisements, billboards, and other print media.

Collective Group Activity: As a collective group, try to recall as many of the infamous Joe Camel ads as possible. Try to recall the details from each of those ads. What was Joe doing? Where was he at? What was in the background? What was he wearing? What did his body look like? Then, discuss the difference between the Joe Camels in those ads and the Joe Chemos below? Give specifics. Are both depicting reality? Why or why not?

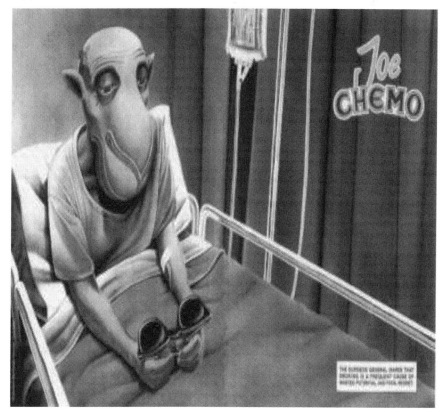

"Courtesy of www.adbusters.org"

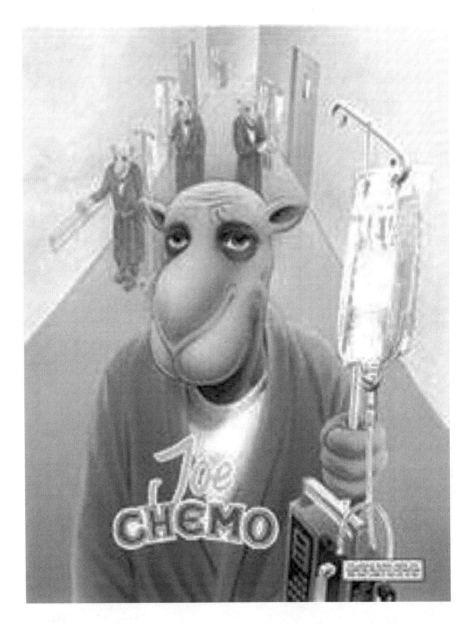

Collaborative Group Activity: Break into small groups and select a magazine. Your job is to find a tobacco advertisement—if you cannot find a tobacco advertisement, find a cologne or expensive makeup advertisement and pick it apart. Tell us why the marketer chose this layout for the ad.

Why does it entice you as a teenager? Give us details. The group will choose a group leader to present to the class.

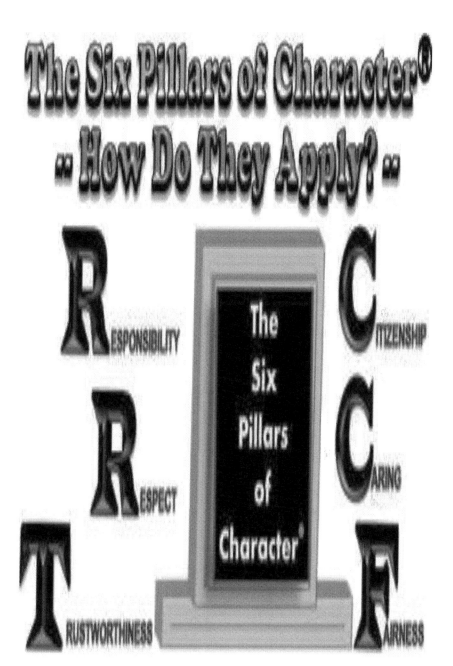

When we began the session, we briefly discussed the Six Pillars of Character as we framed our class values. Being a person of good character isn't always the easy thing to do, but we want to talk about its importance in life.

Character Attributes on Index Cards

What is this thing called character? In order to start thinking through decisions, we must first consider the characteristics we believe are important to be a person of good character. So, let's first decide what is good character?

Collaborative Group Activity:

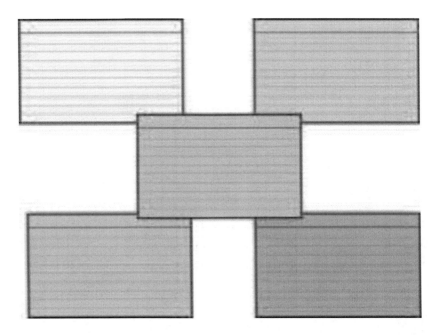

❶ Give each group member 5 index cards.

❷ Pick out an attribute of someone, living or dead, who is a person of good character. In thinking about this person, what characteristic or attribute does this person possess that demonstrates he or she is a person of good character. Write one attribute per index card.

---

3 From the five cards, pick out your three favorites that describe what you personally believe is most important to be a person of good character.

4 Divide the class into two to four small groups. In your small group, share your three favorite attributes and allow each member to do the same. The group should pick out only three of those attributes that describe a person of good character. Show them to the facilitator and receive a piece of easel paper and a set of markers per small group.

5 Each group should then "draw" a representation of each of the three virtues or characteristics without using any words.

6 Then, each group will display their work. The other groups should try to guess what the top three characteristics were. Was their overlap between groups?

How did the group's GOOD CHARACTER attributes compare with this definition below?

Look at the easel paper displays and the attribute each group felt defines a person of character. How did the group's concept compare with the definition below?

> **A person of good character =**
> Someone who is willing to do what is right even when it costs more than he or she may want to pay, (i.e., a friendship, pride, time, or money). It means taking responsibility for one's actions. Some say it's how you behave when no one is looking.

Collective Group Discussion: Let's discuss the quote on the previous page. What do we think the quote means and give specific examples.

Collective Group Discussion: Let's discuss this next quote. What do we think the quote means? Give specific examples.

> **"Our true character is revealed by how we treat people who cannot help or hurt us."**
> --Michael Josephson, Founder
> CHARACTER COUNTS! Coalition

Moral Courage

Collective Group Discussion:

- ❖ Discuss what you think "Moral Courage" means and how it is different from physical courage.
- ❖ Compare your impression of moral courage to the following definitions.

> **Moral courage is the power or will to resist pressure and hold onto important values even in the face of criticism, possible embarrassment, being unpopular, or losing something you want or had.**

People with MORAL COURAGE

Moral Courage

People with MORAL COURAGE have a firmness of spirit that enables them to:

01	02	03	04	05
Try New Things.	Pursue Goals.	Persevere.	Overcome Fears.	Face Problems Head On.

What does this quote mean?

> "In the middle of difficulty lies opportunity."
> --Albert Einstein

How could it apply to your lives now?
How does it apply to MORAL COURAGE?

Circle within a Circle

We are near the end of our MK Journey and we have learned much, grown together, and we are now on our journey toward a tremendously bright future. Facilitator will lead group in a quick review using the "Circle within a Circle" activity.

Now, discuss the following topics, and begin with the person directly in front of you.

* **The main reason you would like to quit using tobacco? (Rotate to the next person.)** Now, discuss the following topics, and begin with the person directly in front of you.

* **What is most embarrassing to you about smoking? (Rotate to the next person.)** Now, discuss the following topics, and begin with the person directly in front of you.

* **Who is the one person you are most ashamed to be around when smoking? (Rotate to the next person.)** Now, discuss the following topics, and begin with the person directly in front of you.

* **Who is the person you would be really embarrassed to face should he or she find out that you smoke? (Rotate to the next person.)**

List the benefits of quitting:

When finished discussing, return to your seat and list the benefits of quitting below. This list could include: Improved health, financial savings, or reasons pertaining to school, social, or work.

❶ _____

❷ _____

❸ _____

❹ _____

❺ _____

To Quit or Not to Quit – Not an Option

If you decide you want to quit smoking or using tobacco, you have to be firm in your decision and stick with it. Even if you find that you can't do it alone, you can stick with your decision to stop. No one has control of your destiny but you. No one can make your decisions for you. No one can make you stick to this decision but you. You are in the driver's seat of your destiny, your health, your life. You have to do it.

So...if you are seriously ready to make a commitment to remain tobacco free...YOU CAN DO IT! If you are not suffering from addiction to nicotine, you are well on your way. The only thing you have to do is choose not to do it again. If you are already suffering from an addiction to tobacco, you may have to fight a little harder—but remember this...The longer you allow your habit to continue, the harder it is to quit!

Collaborative Group Activity: Break into small groups and talk about the "Marlboro Country" picture below. Why is this portraying the "Real Marlboro Country" instead of the usual good-looking men on horses with beautiful scenery? What is the reality of this situation?

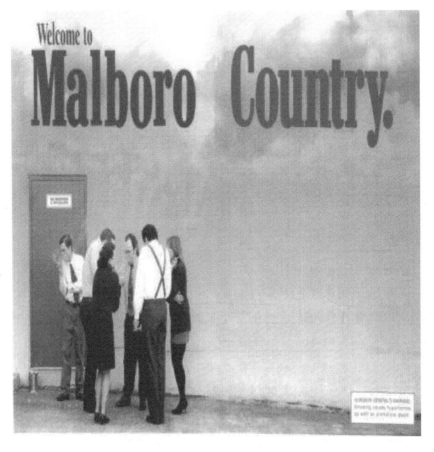

"Courtesy of www.adbusters.org"

The fact is, today almost four out of five people in the USA do not smoke. Think about this: nowadays, **being a nonsmoker is the norm.**

Break into groups of four and discuss the following ways to quit smoking or seek help for the nicotine addiction. Be prepared to discuss your thoughts with the class:

1 **Quitting Cold Turkey** - The majority of people just set a date for when they are going to stop smoking and they stick with it. Some people decide that it is easier just to get it over with and immediately stop.

2 **Modified Cold Turkey** - Others modify plan 1 and set a schedule for tapering off a little each day until they are completely free of tobacco. Whichever you choose—either Plan 1 or Plan 2—set a date and stick with it.

3 **A Physician** - There are medications a physician can prescribe to help in dealing with the withdrawal symptoms that accompany stopping an addictive habit, but your parents must lead you in this process. Speak to your parents about this possibility.

4 Don't forget what you learned about **"Mind Twists and "Logical Thinking."** This may be enough to overcome your addiction, and it may not be. Either way this way of thinking will help you with success in life. If it is not enough to overcome the addiction, seek the help you need whether it be a medical doctor or a psychologist.

5 **Counseling** - There are counselors who can help if all else fails or if you just need a little assistance along the way. You could talk to your school counselor first and/or seek guidance from a professional counselor. Talk to your parents/caregivers for guidance.

Helpful Hints:

1 Exercise is a great way to make you feel great and release endorphins that give a natural high.

2 Find healthy substitutes like snacking on carrots or celery or chew sugarless gum. Start drinking water when you would normally smoke.

3 Work on a list of reasons why you are glad you quit smoking and keep it with you as a reminder.

4 Do not substitute one bad tobacco for another one. Smokeless tobacco like snuff, chewing tobacco and other smoking tobacco like pipes and cigars are very unhealthy, too. Don't trick yourself into substituting one for another.

Do you want to quit? Here are some Helpful Hints:

The following points are advocated by the top quit-smoking products and Patrick Reynolds. (www.notobacco.org/quitting.html)

➤ The first few days, drink LOTS of water and fluids to help flush out the nicotine and other poisons from your body.

➤ Try hard to stay away from alcohol, sugar and coffee the first week or longer, as these tend to stimulate the desire for a cigarette. Try to avoid fatty foods, as your metabolism will slow down a bit without the nicotine, and you may then gain weight.

Do you want to quit? Here are some Helpful Hints:

The following points are advocated by the top quit-smoking products and Patrick Reynolds.
(www.notobacco.org/quitting.html)

➤ The first few days, drink LOTS of water and fluids to help flush out the nicotine and other poisons from your body.

➤ Try hard to stay away from alcohol, sugar and coffee the first week or longer, as these tend to stimulate the desire for a cigarette. Try to avoid fatty foods, as your metabolism will slow down a bit without the nicotine, and you may then gain weight.

➤ In one study, about 25% of quitters found that an oral substitute was invaluable. Another 25% didn't like the idea at all -- they wanted a clean break with cigarettes. The rest weren't certain.

➤ There is a lot of controversy surrounding E-Cigarettes (Electronic cigarettes). Some view it as a gateway away from using tobacco products. Some view it as a gateway toward using tobacco products in the first place. What do you think?

➤ A rather simpler way to go is to buy bottled cinnamon sticks at the supermarket. Just chew on them and keep them handy, and handle them just like a cigarette. When they get chewed on one end and start looking like an exploded firecracker, chew on the other end. And if people ask, "Excuse me, but is that an exploded firecracker in your mouth?" just tell them you're quitting smoking – and their odd stares will quickly turn to support. You won't need the cinnamon sticks after the first few days of being a nonsmoker.

➢ THIS IS KEY: Every time you want a cigarette, do the following process three times: Inhale deeply and slowly exhale. As you very slowly let the air out, close your eyes and let your chin gradually fall down onto your chest. As you exhale, imagine all the tension leaving your body, just flowing right out of your fingers and toes. This is a variation of an ancient yoga technique from India, and is VERY relaxing. Try it now and see!

➢ Go to a gym, sit in the steam, exercise! Change your normal routine. Take time to walk or even jog around the block or in a local park. Look in the yellow pages under Yoga, and take a class – they're GREAT! Get a one-hour massage, take a long bath— pamper yourself.

➢ Ask for support from friends and family members. Request tolerance, and explain you're quitting, and you might be edgy and grumpy for the first few days. If you don't ask for support, you certainly won't get any. If you do, you'll be surprised how much it can help. Take a chance— try it and see!

➢ It's critically important to ask your smoking friends not to smoke around you—and don't be afraid to ask. If you don't speak up for yourself, no one's going to do it for you. Your friends can't read your mind.

➢ Write down ten good things about being a nonsmoker.

➢ Then, write out ten bad things about smoking. Do it. It really helps.

➢ Don't pretend smoking wasn't enjoyable – it was. This is like losing a good friend – and it's okay to grieve the loss. Feel that grief, don't worry, it's okay. And, as with all losses— feel, and you will heal. Don't anesthetize the pain with food, drugs, alcohol—or you'll just postpone the pain. (For more on this, see the paragraph below which begins, "America is a nation of addicts...").

➢ Several times a day, repeat the affirmation, "I am a nonsmoker." Many quitters see themselves as smokers who are just not smoking at the moment. They think of themselves as smokers who still want a cigarette! Repeating the affirmation "I am a nonsmoker" helps change your own view of yourself, and it is useful. Use it!

➢ Support groups like Nicotine Anonymous might initially seem unnecessary— but they provide a GREAT outlet to verbally vent your suffering. This will spare your family and friends some grumpiness when you are home. And it's therapeutic— really— to see how other quitters are doing in their struggles to stop. Try finding them through 800 information, 1-800-555-1212, or ask your local directory assistance.

Studies show that one reason teens make bad decisions like using tobacco or doing drugs and alcohol is because they are worried about their futures. Worrying about your future is normal because there is much change that occurs as you grow to become an adult and have to make decisions that will affect the rest of your lives.

Positive Thinking

A part of being a responsible person is choosing to respond positively to life and its obstacles.

Why be positive?

First of all, you have a wonderful future ahead of you if you make good decisions. Things may be scary now, but as you grow, you will have wondrous times. There will be unbelievable memories and a whole life to live with precious family, friends, and college or work associates.

Secondly, there is power in your thoughts! We learned this already with Logical Thinking and Mind Twists. We need to think positively, which will lead to our heart in the form of our feelings and then eventually effect our actions. If we are positive from the source, our minds, it will lead to positive actions.

How many times have we been around that person who is so negative about everything we just want to run for the mountains? That is not who we want to be. We want to be that person who shares positive energy and, thus, has it coming back to us.

So then, if there is power in your thoughts, there must also be power in your words. Therefore, be not only thoughtful about what's forming in your mind, but about what you are saying. Learn to turn those negative thoughts and words into positive thoughts and words.

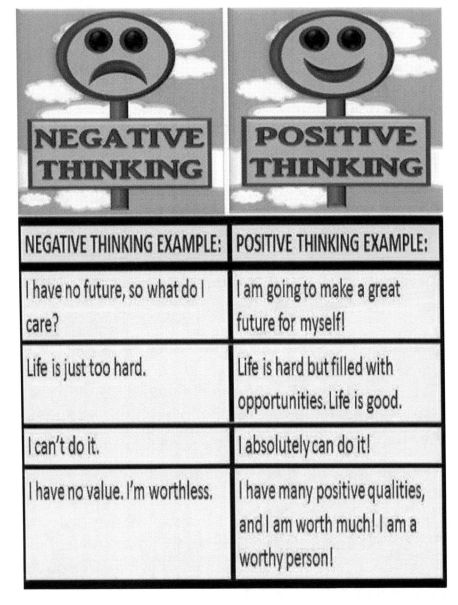

NEGATIVE THINKING EXAMPLE:	POSITIVE THINKING EXAMPLE:
I have no future, so what do I care?	I am going to make a great future for myself!
Life is just too hard.	Life is hard but filled with opportunities. Life is good.
I can't do it.	I absolutely can do it!
I have no value. I'm worthless.	I have many positive qualities, and I am worth much! I am a worthy person!

Talk about your Problems

In order to overcome anxiety, depression, fear, negative thinking, and many other feelings that are not always so positive, it is important to talk about your problems. **NEVER ISOLATE YOURSELF!**

Many times, we feel like just keeping our problems to ourselves, because we feel like no one really cares anyway; and even if they did, they would never understand. These are normal feelings for teens.

Go to someone who will listen and genuinely cares about you and tell them about your feelings. If you feel you don't have someone like that, then go to a counselor at school or with a religious establishment, or call a help-line. Just remember, **you are not alone,** and there are people out there who have felt similar feelings and who care about what happens to you.

There is always a brighter tomorrow — **Never forget that!**

Always remember though what a true friend really is. **A true friend is someone who would never lead you to danger.** Avoid any friend who asks you to participate in risky behavior.

To talk is to heal. To keep your feelings inside is like a pressure tank gaining more and more pressure and eventually an explosion of some kind will occur. There is always someone out there who cares about you!

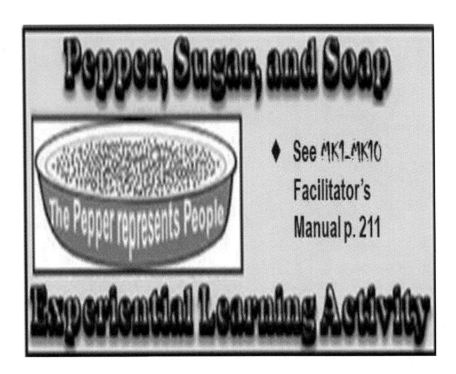

Collective Group Activity: The Power of Thoughts—Just Believe!

Each participant will be given a 12″ string with a small washer (or individually wrapped lifesaver) tied to the end.

Each participant will hold the string so the washer is straight across from their nose. They are NOT to move their hand at all.

---

❶ Now, looking at the washer, each participant is to think, **"LEFT, RIGHT, LEFT, RIGHT."** The facilitator will keep saying this slowly and encouraging participants not to move their hand.

❷ Now, The facilitator will say, "Now think, **FRONT, BACK, FRONT, BACK** again and again." while encouraging participants not to move their hands. By this time, most will be getting their washer to move as they are thinking.

❸ Finally, the facilitator will ask the participants to think **"CIRCLE, CIRCLE, CIRCLE."** Many will be able to get their washer going in a circle.

Facilitator asks the following four questions:

➲ What did you observe happening?

➲ Why did the washer move? (Hint: The power of our mind actually sends the message to our hand and it moved, but we aren't conscious of that. It is the power of believing, of thinking that makes it happen.)

➲ How does this activity apply to quitting smoking? (Hint: You have to believe you can do it and stay confident— getting the help you need for any true addiction to nicotine).

➲ How does this activity apply to R.E.B.T. and making decisions in all areas of your lives?

(Adapted from Tom Jackson. www.activelearning.com)

Florence Chadwick & Goal-Setting

FLorence CHadWick Story

♦ See MK1-MK10 Facilitator's Manual pp. 157-162

Create a Commitment Collage

Collective Group Activity: Group Commitment Collage

There will be a sticky sheet or piece of easel paper for the entire group to create a "Commitment Collage". Each person will add at least one new commitment to the Collage in the form of a word, symbol, statement, etc. However, the object is to create a piece of art. It is possible that your group could win a poster contest and even a stipend from the founders of MK — Foundations for Life Principles.

(Providers are urged to send photos of these to FLP quarterly.)

Collective Group Discussion: End with a discussion on the following quote.

"Optimism is the faith that leads to achievement. Nothing can be done without hope and confidence."
--Helen Keller

Dear Carrie,

OR

Dear FLP,

Write a feedback letter about MK experience to FLP - Foundations for Life Principles Author: Carrie D. Marchant

♦ See MK1_MK10 Facilitator's Manual pp. 131-134

Contacts in Times of Need

American Cancer Society www.cancer.org	1-800-227-2345
www.tobaccofreekids.org 1400 Eye Street N.W. – Suite 1200 Washington, DC 20005	1-866-435-7825 1-202-296-5469
Nicotine Anonymous http://www.nicotine-anonymous.org/	1-877-TRYNICA (1-877-879-6422)
Al-Anon/Alateen Hotline Hope & Help for young people who are the relatives & friends of a problem drinker.	1-888-425-2666 6
Al-Anon Family Group Headquarters, Inc. For those who have been affected by someone else's alcohol or drug problems; also based on the AA model. http://www.al-anon.alateen.org/ ; https://chat.alateen.net/ e-mail: wso@al-anon.org	1-888-425-2666
Alcoholics Anonymous The original 12-step self-help program, with free meeting in nearly every community. http://www.aa.org/	1-212-870-3400 (M-F, 8:30 am- 4:45 pm EST)
Center for Substance Abuse Treatment Substance Abuse and Mental Health Services Administration Referral Service: http://beta.samhsa.gov/	1-877-SAMHSA- 7 (877-726-4727) 1-800-487-4889 (M-F, 8:30 am- 5:00 pm EST)
National Suicide Prevention Hotline http://www.suicidepreventionlifeline.org/ https://www.facebook.com/800273TALK	1-800-273-TALK 1-800-273-8255

Unpleasant Feeling Words

Angry	Depressed	Confused	Helpless
irritated	lousy	upset	incapable
enraged	disappointed	doubtful	alone
upset	discouraged	uncertain	paralyzed
insulted	ashamed	indecisive	fatigued
annoyed	powerless	perplexed	useless
hateful	guilty	embarrassed	inferior
unpleasant	dissatisfied	hesitant	vulnerable
offensive	miserable	shy	empty
bitter	disgusting	disillusioned	forced
aggressive	terrible	unbelieving	hesitant
resentful	in despair	skeptical	despair
provoked	sulky	distrusting	frustrated
infuriated	bad	lost	distressed
worked up	a sense of loss	unsure	woeful
boiling		uneasy	pathetic
fuming		pessimistic	dominated
		tense	
		uneasy	

Indifferent	Afraid	Hurt	Sad
insensitive	fearful	crushed	tearful
dull	terrified	tormented	sorrowful
nonchalant	suspicious	deprived	pained
neutral	anxious	pained	grief
reserved	panic	tortured	anguish
weary	nervous	rejected	desolate
bored	scared	injured	desperate
preoccupied	worried	offended	pessimistic
cold	frightened	afflicted	unhappy
disinterested	timid	aching	lonely
lifeless	shaky	victimized	grieved
	restless	heartbroken	mournful
	doubtful	agonized	dismayed
	threatened	appalled	
	cowardly	humiliated	
	wary	wronged	
		alienated	

Pleasant Feeling Words

Open	Happy	Alive	Good
understanding	great	playful	calm
confident	elated	courageous	peaceful
reliable	joyous	energetic	at ease
easy	lucky	liberated	comfortable
amazed	fortunate	optimistic	pleased
free	delighted	provocative	encouraged
sympathetic	overjoyed	impulsive	clever
interested	gleeful	free	surprised
satisfied	thankful	frisky	content
receptive	important	animated	quiet
accepting	festive	spirited	certain
kind	ecstatic	thrilled	relaxed
	satisfied	wonderful	serene
	glad		free and easy
	cheerful		bright
	sunny		blessed
	merry		reassured

Love	Interested	Positive	Strong
loving	concerned	eager	impulsive
considerate	affected	intent	free
affectionate	fascinated	anxious	sure
sensitive	intrigued	inspired	certain
tender	absorbed	determined	rebellious
devoted	inquisitive	excited	unique
attracted	nosy	enthusiastic	dynamic
passionate	snoopy	bold	secure
admiration	curious	brave	tenacious
warm		daring	
touched		challenged	
sympathy		optimistic	
close		re-enforced	
loved		confident	
comforted		hopeful	

Made in the USA
Columbia, SC
21 December 2022

73040484R00057